Brussel Sprouts Recipes

A Brussel Sprouts Cookbook with Delicious Brussels Sprouts Recipes

By
BookSumo Press

Published by
http://www.booksumo.com

Table of Contents

How to Braise
Brussel Sprouts

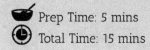 Prep Time: 5 mins
Total Time: 15 mins

Servings per Recipe: 4
Calories	163.5
Fat	14.0g
Cholesterol	0.0mg
Sodium	24.4mg
Carbohydrates	8.8g
Protein	3.0g

Ingredients
1 lb. Brussels sprout
4 - 6 tbsp extra-virgin olive oil
3 - 4 garlic cloves, minced
lemon juice
salt
white pepper

Directions
1. Discard the brown leaves of the brussels sprouts. Slice them in half.
2. Place a heavy saucepan over medium heat. Heat in it the oil.
3. Cook in it the brussels sprouts for 8 to 10 min until they become golden brown while stirring.
4. Stir in the garlic and cook them for one minute.
5. Add the lemon juice with a pinch of salt and pepper. Toss them to coat and serve them warm.
6. Enjoy.

RED BELL
Brussel Sprouts

🥣 Prep Time: 20 mins
🕐 Total Time: 40 mins

Servings per Recipe: 6
Calories   187.6
Fat   12.1g
Cholesterol   30.5mg
Sodium   121.1mg
Carbohydrates   18.5g
Protein   5.8g

Ingredients
2 lbs. Brussels sprouts, trimmed
2 red bell peppers, seeded, sliced
1 onions, sliced
2 garlic cloves, minced
6 tbsp butter
salt
pepper
2 tbsp lemon juice

Directions
1. Use a sharp knife to make a cut in the shape of X in the bottom of each brussels sprout.
2. Place a large skillet over medium heat. Heat in it the butter.
3. Cook in it the garlic with pepper and onion for 4 min.
4. Stir in the brussels sprouts with a pinch of salt and pepper. Cook them for 4 to 6 min.
5. Stir in the lemon rind then serve them warm.
6. Enjoy.

Lover's
Brussel Sprouts

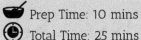 Prep Time: 10 mins

Total Time: 25 mins

Servings per Recipe: 2
Calories	229.2
Fat	19.5g
Cholesterol	22.9mg
Sodium	110.0mg
Carbohydrates	12.6g
Protein	4.3g

Ingredients
15 Brussels sprouts halved lengthwise
1 1/2 tbsp butter
1 1/2 tbsp olive oil
3 cloves garlic, smashed with the flat of a
knife
 grated parmesan cheese
salt and pepper

Directions
1. Place a large pan over medium heat. Heat in the oil with butter.
2. Lower the heat and add the garlic. Fry it for 1 to 2 min until it becomes brown.
3. Drain it and discard it. Stir in the brussels sprouts and cook them for 12 to 16 min until they become soft.
4. Season them with a pinch of salt and pepper. Garnish them with parmesan cheese then serve them warm.
5. Enjoy.

THAI STYLE
Brussel Sprouts

Prep Time: 10 mins
Total Time: 25 mins

Servings per Recipe: 3
Calories	185.0
Fat	14.3g
Cholesterol	0.0mg
Sodium	730.9mg
Carbohydrates	12.0g
Protein	5.3g

Ingredients
1 lb. Brussels sprout, trimmed and halved
3 tbsp olive oil
2 tbsp low sodium soy sauce
1 tbsp sriracha sauce
1 1/2 tsp Dijon mustard
1/2 tsp ground ginger
1 tsp chopped garlic
sesame seeds

Directions
1. Get a mixing bowl: Whisk in it the olive oil, soy sauce, Sriracha, mustard, ginger, and garlic powder.
2. Add the brussels sprouts and toss them to coat. Let them sit for 5 to 7 min.
3. Place a large pot over high heat.
4. Add to it the brussels sprouts mixture and cook them for 10 to 14 min while occasionally stirring.
5. Garnish them with sesame seeds then serve them warm.
6. Enjoy.

Brussel Sprouts
with Cannellini

🍲 Prep Time: 20 mins
🕐 Total Time: 40 mins

Servings per Recipe: 8
Calories   254.4
Fat   17.2g
Cholesterol   7.6mg
Sodium   61.4mg
Carbohydrates   20.4g
Protein   7.5g

Ingredients

8 tbsp extra-virgin olive oil, divided
2 lbs. Brussels sprouts, trimmed, halved lengthwise
6 garlic cloves, chopped
1 C. low sodium chicken broth
1 (15 oz.) cans cannellini, drained
2 tbsp butter

1 C. grated pecorino cheese

Directions

1. Place a large pan over medium heat. Heat in it 3 tbsp of oil.
2. Stir in it 1 lb. of brussels sprouts and cook them for 6 min while stirring often.
3. Drain them and transfer them to a mixing bowl.
4. Repeat the process with another 3 tbsp of oil and the remaining brussels sprouts.
5. Heat 2 tbsp of oil in the same pan Fry in it the garlic on high heat for 60 sec while stirring.
6. Stir in the cooked brussels sprouts with broth.
7. Cook them for 4 min. Stir in the butter with beans. Cook them for 2 min while stirring.
8. Adjust the seasoning of your stir fry then serve it warm.
9. Enjoy.

BUTTERY
Balsamic Sprout Bowls

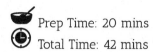
Prep Time: 20 mins
Total Time: 42 mins

Servings per Recipe: 16
Calories	77.4
Fat	3.0g
Cholesterol	7.6mg
Sodium	149.6mg
Carbohydrates	11.8g
Protein	1.9g

Ingredients
2 3/4 lb. small Brussels sprouts, trimmed
and cleaned
1/2 C. sugar
1/4 C. butter
1/4 C. apple cider vinegar
1/4 C. balsamic vinegar
3/4 C. water
3/4 tsp salt

Directions
1. Place a dutch oven over high heat. Stir in it the sugar until it starts melting.
2. Lower the heat and let it cook while stirring until it melts.
3. Stir in the butter until it melts. Pour in the apple cider and balsamic vinegar. Stir them well for 1 min.
4. Stir in the salt with water. Heat them until they start boiling.
5. Stir in the Brussels sprouts and bring them to another boil.
6. Lower the heat and put on the lid. Cook them for 7 min.
7. Remove the lid and let them cook for an extra 16 min while stirring them often.
8. Serve your sweet brussels sprouts warm.
9. Enjoy.

Backyard
Brussel Sprouts

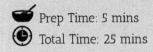

Prep Time: 5 mins
Total Time: 25 mins

Servings per Recipe: 6
Calories   42.2
Fat   2.5g
Cholesterol   0.0mg
Sodium   12.1mg
Carbohydrates   4.4g
Protein   1.5g

Ingredients
1 tbsp olive oil
2 large garlic cloves, minced
3/4 lb. Brussels sprout, trimmed, leaves
pulled off, cores quartered
1/8 tsp lemon pepper
1/8 sea salt
1 tsp lemon zest, minced

Directions
1. Place a large saucepan over medium heat. Heat in it the oil.
2. Cook in it the garlic for 40 sec. Lower the heat and stir in the brussels sprouts.
3. Cook them for 10 to 12 min while stirring them often.
4. Once the time is up, stir in 2 tbsp of water and put on the lid. Cook them for 6 min.
5. Stir in the lemon zest with a pinch of salt and pepper. Serve them warm.
6. Enjoy.

BRUSSEL SPROUTS
on the Grill

Prep Time: 5 mins
Total Time: 15 mins

Servings per Recipe: 4
Calories	108.1
Fat	11.5g
Cholesterol	30.5mg
Sodium	102.7mg
Carbohydrates	1.3g
Protein	0.5g

Ingredients
14 oz. frozen Brussels sprouts, thawed
1/4 C. butter, melted
1/2 tsp garlic salt
1/2 tsp onion powder

Directions
1. Before you do anything, preheat the grill and grease it.
2. Get a mixing bowl: Whisk in it the butter with garlic and onion powder.
3. Thread the brussels sprouts onto skewers.
4. Grill them for 8 to 10 min while turning them and basting them with the butter mixture.
5. Serve them warm with a sauce of your choice.
6. Enjoy.

Lemony Agave
Brussel Sprouts

🥣 Prep Time: 10 mins
🕐 Total Time: 40 mins

Servings per Recipe: 4
Calories   171.4
Fat   14.3g
Cholesterol   0.0mg
Sodium   109.9mg
Carbohydrates   9.8g
Protein   3.4g

Ingredients
1 lb. Brussels sprout, trimmed
1/4 C. extra-virgin olive oil
1/4 C. agave nectar
2 tbsp mustard
2 tbsp minced garlic
1 lemon, juice

Directions
1. Before you do anything, preheat the oven to 350 F.
2. Cover a baking tray with foil. Place it aside.
3. Get a large mixing bowl: Whisk in it the oil with agave, mustard, and garlic.
4. Add the brussels sprouts with a pinch of salt and pepper. Stir them to coat.
5. Spoon the mixture to the tray and bake it for 15 min.
6. Flip the brussels sprouts and bake them for an extra 15 min.
7. Drizzle over them the lemon juice then serve them warm.
8. Enjoy.

SWEET
Saskatoon Style Sprouts

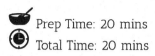 Prep Time: 20 mins
Total Time: 20 mins

Servings per Recipe: 10
Calories	244.8
Fat	16.8g
Cholesterol	24.4mg
Sodium	24.8mg
Carbohydrates	22.8g
Protein	3.1g

Ingredients
1/4 C. canola oil
2 1/4 lbs. baby Brussels sprouts, trimmed
and halved lengthwise
salt & ground black pepper
1/2 C. unsalted butter, chopped and
softened
2 tbsp light brown sugar
1/4 C. grade a pure maple syrup
1 1/2 tbsp cider vinegar

1 C. vacuum-packed roasted chestnuts,
chopped
1 tbsp walnut oil

Directions
1. Place a large pan over high heat. Heat in it the canola oil.
2. Stir in it the brussels sprouts with a pinch of salt and pepper. Cook them for 2 min.
3. Stir in the brown sugar with butter. Cook them until the butter melts.
4. Stir in the maple syrup and let them cook for 8 min while stirring them often.
5. Once the time is up, add the vinegar with chestnuts and walnut oil.
6. Drain the brussels sprouts and transfer them to a serving plate.
7. Cook the remaining sauce in the pan for 2 to 3 min until it becomes thick.
8. Drizzle it over the brussels sprouts then serve them warm.
9. Enjoy.

Brussel Sprout
Mash

Prep Time: 10 mins
Total Time: 30 mins

Servings per Recipe: 4
Calories	546.4
Fat	39.4g
Cholesterol	132.2mg
Sodium	679.6mg
Carbohydrates	30.1g
Protein	25.4g

Ingredients

1 1/2 kg Brussels sprouts, trimmed and
cleaned
284 ml double cream
150 g parmesan cheese, grated
salt and pepper

Directions

1. Before you do anything, preheat the oven to 350 F.
2. Bring a large salted pot of water to a boil. Cook in it the brussels sprouts for 5 min.
3. Drain them and transfer them to a food processor with cream, a pinch of salt and pepper.
4. Pulse them several times until they become chopped.
5. Pour the mixture into a baking dish and stir into it third of the parmesan cheese.
6. Sprinkle the rest of the cheese on top.
7. Bake them for 5 to 6 min until the cheese melts then serve them warm.
8. Enjoy.

MS. WONG'S
Potluck Brussel Sprouts

☕ Prep Time: 10 mins
🕐 Total Time: 35 mins

Servings per Recipe: 6
Calories   103.5
Fat   5.6g
Cholesterol   0.0mg
Sodium   199.7mg
Carbohydrates   11.7g
Protein   4.5g

Ingredients

2 lbs. Brussels sprouts, washed, trimmed
with x cut on the bottom
1 1/2 tbsp peanut oil
1 - 2 tsp minced garlic
1/2 tbsp grated gingerroot
1 tbsp soy sauce
1/2-1 tsp crushed red pepper flakes
1/4 tsp black pepper
1/4 tsp sugar

1 tbsp sesame seeds
1 tsp sesame oil

Directions

1. Bring a large salted pot of water to a boil. Cook in it the brussels sprouts for 8 to 12 min.

2. Drain them and place them aside.

3. Place a large pan over medium heat. Combine in it the ginger with garlic and peanut oil.

4. Cook them for 2 min. Add the soy sauce, crushed red pepper, black pepper, sugar and sesame seeds.

5. Add the brussels sprouts with a pinch of salt and pepper. Cook them for 6 to 8 min.

6. Drizzle over them the sesame oil then serves them warm.

7. Enjoy.

Lemon Pepper
Brussel Sprouts

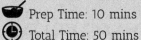 Prep Time: 10 mins
Total Time: 50 mins

Servings per Recipe: 6
Calories   101.0
Fat   7.3g
Cholesterol   0.0mg
Sodium   217.8mg
Carbohydrates   8.1g
Protein   2.9g

Ingredients
1 1/2 lbs. Brussels sprouts, trimmed and
cleaned
3 tbsp olive oil
1/2-3/4 tsp kosher salt
1/2 tsp lemon-pepper seasoning

Directions
1. Before you do anything, preheat the oven to 400 F.
2. Get a large mixing bowl: Stir in it the brussels sprouts with olive oil, salt, and lemon
   pepper seasoning.
3. Spread the mixture on a baking sheet. Bake it for 36 to 42 min. Serve them warm.
4. Enjoy.

BRUSSEL SPROUTS
University Heights

Prep Time: 10 mins
Total Time: 25 mins

Servings per Recipe: 6
Calories   107.1
Fat   5.7g
Cholesterol   13.8mg
Sodium   122.8mg
Carbohydrates   11.0g
Protein   5.5g

Ingredients
2 lbs. Brussels sprouts, trimmed
2 tbsp butter
1 garlic clove, crushed
1/4 C. grated parmesan cheese

Directions
1. Bring a large salted pot of water to a boil. Cook in it the brussels sprouts for 9 min.
2. Drain them and place them aside.
3. Place a large saucepan over medium heat. Stir in it the butter with garlic.
4. Cook them for 1 min. Add the brussels sprouts with a pinch of salt and pepper.
5. Cook them for 2 min then transfer them to a serving plate. Garnish them with cheese then serve them warm.
6. Enjoy.

Oven Fried
Brussel Sprouts

🥣 Prep Time: 20 mins
🕐 Total Time: 35 mins

Servings per Recipe: 10
Calories	105.2
Fat	7.9g
Cholesterol	20.0mg
Sodium	359.5mg
Carbohydrates	6.9g
Protein	2.9g

Ingredients

1 1/2 lbs. Brussels sprouts, trimmed
2 - 3 C. cold water
1 tsp salt
6 tbsp butter, melted, divided
4 tbsp grated parmesan cheese
4 tbsp dry breadcrumbs
1/4 tsp granulated garlic powder

1/4 tsp ground black pepper
1/4 tsp seasoning salt

Directions

1. Use a sharp knife to make two cuts in the shape of an X at the bottom of each Brussels sprout.
2. Bring a large salted saucepan of water to a boil. Cook in it the brussels sprouts with the lid on for 7 min.
3. Drain them and transfer them to a baking dish. Add 3 tbsp of butter with a pinch of salt and pepper.
4. Stir them to coat and spread them into an even layer.
5. Get a mixing bowl: Mix in it the Parmesan cheese, dried bread crumbs, granulated garlic powder, black pepper, seasoning salt and remaining butter.
6. Spread the mixture over the brussels sprouts. Bake it for 5 to 6 min.
7. Serve your brussels sprouts casserole warm.
8. Enjoy.

BABY
Brussel Sprouts

Prep Time: 10 mins
Total Time: 45 mins

Servings per Recipe: 4
Calories	60.1
Fat	2.6g
Cholesterol	0.0mg
Sodium	56.2mg
Carbohydrates	8.7g
Protein	1.8g

Ingredients
1/2 lb. baby carrots, whole, par cooked
1/2 lb. Brussels sprout, trimmed and par
cooked
2 tsp olive oil
salt and pepper

Directions
1. Before you do anything preheat the oven to 400 F.
2. Bring a large salted pot of water to a boil. Cook in it the brussels sprouts for 7 min.
3. Drain them and transfer them to a casserole dish. Add the carrot with oil, a pinch of salt and pepper.
4. Stir them to coat and bake them for 22 min. Serve it warm.
5. Enjoy.

Picnic
Brussel Sprouts

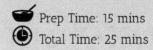

Prep Time: 15 mins
Total Time: 25 mins

Servings per Recipe: 6
Calories	112.3
Fat	8.2g
Cholesterol	20.3mg
Sodium	91.6mg
Carbohydrates	9.3g
Protein	3.0g

Ingredients
1 1/2 lbs. Brussels sprouts, strips
1/4 C. butter
2 limes, juice
salt
pepper

Directions
1. Place a large pan over high heat. Heat in it the butter until it melts.
2. Add the brussels sprouts and cook them for 7 to 11 min.
3. Turn off the heat and add the lime juice with a pinch of salt and pepper.
4. Serve them warm.
5. Enjoy.

HAPPY 30
Brussel Sprouts

🥣 Prep Time: 5 mins
🕐 Total Time: 30 mins

Servings per Recipe: 4
Calories	116.9
Fat	4.5g
Cholesterol	0.0mg
Sodium	204.6mg
Carbohydrates	17.8g
Protein	3.9g

Ingredients
1 lb. Brussels sprout, trimmed
1 tbsp olive oil
1/3 C. minced shallot
1/2 tsp salt
1/3 C. water
1/4 C. mustard
2 tbsp brown sugar
ground black pepper

Directions
1. Slice off the base of the brussels sprouts then cut each one of them into 5 slices.
2. Place a large pan over medium heat. Heat in it the oil.
3. Sauté in it the shallot for 3 min. Add the brussels sprouts with 3 tbsp of water and a pinch of salt.
4. Spread the mixture in the pan, lower the heat and put on the lid. Let them cook for 6 min.
5. Get a mixing bowl: Whisk in it the mustard, brown sugar, and remaining water.
6. Stir the mixture into the pan. Lower the heat and put on the lid. Cook them for 7 min while stirring often.
7. Serve your glazed brussels sprouts warm.
8. Enjoy.

Waldorf
Brussel Sprouts

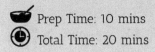 Prep Time: 10 mins

Total Time: 20 mins

Servings per Recipe: 4

Calories	130.8
Fat	8.9g
Cholesterol	3.6mg
Sodium	181.5mg
Carbohydrates	9.5g
Protein	5.9g

Ingredients
1 lb. Brussels sprout, trimmed and quartered
2 tsp walnut oil
1 garlic clove, minced
4 tbsp vegetable broth
1/8 tsp salt
1/8 tsp ground allspice
pepper
1/4 C. chopped walnuts
1/4 C. grated Parmigiano-Reggiano cheese

Directions
1. Place a large pan over medium heat. Heat in it the oil.
2. Cook in it the sprouts, garlic, salt, allspice and pepper for 3 min.
3. Stir in the broth and cook them for 8 to 9 min until it evaporates.
4. Add the walnuts with a pinch of salt and pepper.
5. Transfer them to a serving dish and top them with cheese.
6. Enjoy.

HAZELNUT
Brussel Sprouts

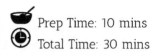

Prep Time: 10 mins
Total Time: 30 mins

Servings per Recipe: 4
Calories	119.3
Fat	8.5g
Cholesterol	7.6mg
Sodium	194.8mg
Carbohydrates	9.4g
Protein	4.1g

Ingredients
1 tbsp butter
1 lb. Brussels sprout, trimmed and quartered
1/4 C. chopped hazelnuts
1/4 tsp salt
ground pepper
3 tbsp water

Directions
1. Before you do anything, preheat the oven to 450 F.
2. Place the butter in a baking tray. Cook it in the oven for 3 min.
3. Pull it out and add to it the brussels sprouts with hazelnuts, a pinch of salt and pepper.
4. Stir them to coat and bake them for another 6 to 8 min.
5. Add the water and cook them for another 8 min. Serve them warm.
6. Enjoy.

Korean
Brussel Sprouts

🥘 Prep Time: 15 mins
🕐 Total Time: 30 mins

Servings per Recipe: 8
Calories   56.0
Fat   2.6g
Cholesterol   0.0mg
Sodium   267.2mg
Carbohydrates   7.1g
Protein   2.5g

Ingredients

2 (10 oz.) containers Brussels sprouts, trimmed and quartered
2 tbsp soy sauce
2 tsp ginger, peeled & grated
1 tsp sesame oil
1 tbsp olive oil
1 large onion, halved & sliced

2 tbsp water

Directions

1. Get a mixing bowl: Whisk in it the soy sauce, grated ginger, and sesame oil.
2. Place a large pan over medium heat. Heat in it the oil.
3. Sauté in it the onion for 4 min. Add the brussels sprouts and cook them over high heat for 6 min with the lid on.
4. Once the time is up,, remove the lid and cook them for an extra 4 min while stirring them often.
5. Add the sauce mixture and cook them for 1 min.
6. Adjust the seasoning of your brussels sprouts then serve them warm.
7. Enjoy.

MAPLE GLAZED
Brussel Sprouts

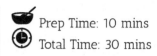

Prep Time: 10 mins
Total Time: 30 mins

Servings per Recipe: 4
Calories   170.3
Fat   11.4g
Cholesterol   0.0mg
Sodium   24.1mg
Carbohydrates   17.4g
Protein   1.5g

Ingredients
1/4 C. pecan halves, trimmed and halved
1/4 lb. Brussels sprout
2 oz. white pearl onions, tip, and root ends
cut off
1/2 C. water
1/4 C. maple syrup
1 tsp Dijon mustard
2 tbsp extra virgin olive oil
salt and pepper

Directions
1. Before you do anything, preheat the oven to 350 F.
2. Place the pecans on a lined up baking tray. Bake them for 7 to 8 min.
3. Place them aside and let them cool down completely.
4. Place a heavy saucepan of water over high heat. Heat in it until it starts boiling.
5. Cook in it the onions for 60 sec. Drain them, peel them and place them aside.
6. Get a mixing bowl: Whisk in it the water, maple syrup, and mustard.
7. Place a large pan over medium heat. Heat in it the oil.
8. Cook in it the onions with brussels sprouts for 4 min.
9. Stir in the maple mixture and cook them for 11 to 14 min over low heat.
10. Add the pecans with a pinch of salt and pepper. Serve them hot.
11. Enjoy.

Brussels Sprouts
Genesee

Prep Time: 10 mins
Total Time: 30 mins

Servings per Recipe: 6
Calories	223.4
Fat	18.0g
Cholesterol	30.5mg
Sodium	144.5mg
Carbohydrates	14.0g
Protein	4.9g

Ingredients
1 lb. Brussels sprout, cleaned and outer
leaves removed
1/2 lb. carrot, cleaned and sliced
6 tbsp butter
1 tbsp brown sugar
1 tbsp lemon juice
salt

pepper
1/2 C. chives, chopped
1/2 C. toasted almond

Directions
1. Bring a large salted pot of water to a boil. Cook in it the brussels sprouts and cook them for 11 min.
2. Stir in the carrots and let them cook for 5 min. Drain them all and place them aside.
3. Place a large pan over medium heat. Stir in it the butter with sugar and lemon juice for 1 min.
4. Stir in the carrots with brussels sprouts. Cook them for 6 min while stirring.
5. Adjust the seasoning of your veggies then stirs in the chives with almonds. Serve them hot.
6. Enjoy.

BRUSSEL SPROUTS
in College

Prep Time: 10 mins
Total Time: 25 mins

Servings per Recipe: 2
Calories	107.3
Fat	4.1g
Cholesterol	0.0mg
Sodium	32.5mg
Carbohydrates	16.1g
Protein	4.4g

Ingredients

10 oz. Brussels sprouts, trimmed and sliced
1 medium onion, sliced
2 garlic cloves, minced
1/2 tbsp olive oil
salt and pepper

Directions

1. Before you do anything, preheat the oven to 450 F.
2. Get a large mixing bowl: Toss in it the brussels sprouts with onion, garlic, oil, a pinch of salt and pepper.
3. Spread the mixture on a lined up baking tray. Bake them for 16 min while stirring them halfway through cooking.
4. Serve them warm with some roasted meat.
5. Enjoy.

Twin City
Chunked Vegetable Roast

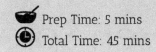

Prep Time: 5 mins
Total Time: 45 mins

Servings per Recipe: 6
Calories   288.6
Fat   10.1g
Cholesterol   0.0mg
Sodium   128.5mg
Carbohydrates   46.3g
Protein   7.5g

Ingredients
28 oz. potatoes, chunks
28 oz. Brussels sprouts, trimmed
28 oz. carrots, peeled and cut into chunks
1/4 C. olive oil
2 tbsp thyme leaves
4 garlic cloves, crushed

Directions
1. Before you do anything, preheat the oven to 450 F.
2. Get a large mixing bowl: Stir in the brussels sprouts, potatoes, carrots, oil, thyme, a pinch of salt and pepper.
3. Transfer the mixture to a roasting pan. Bake them for 22 min.
4. Stir in the garlic and bake them for an extra 22 min.
5. Serve them warm.
6. Enjoy.

25-MINUTE
Oven Sprouts

Prep Time: 5 mins
Total Time: 25 mins

Servings per Recipe: 2
Calories   146.7
Fat   4.6g
Cholesterol   2.2mg
Sodium   369.7mg
Carbohydrates   22.8g
Protein   7.7g

Ingredients
10 oz. fresh Brussels sprouts
1 whole garlic, cloves separated and peeled
1 1/2 tsp olive oil
1/2 tsp lemon pepper
1/4 tsp sea salt
1 tbsp grated parmesan cheese

Directions
1. Before you do anything, preheat the oven to 400 F.
2. Get a mixing bowl: Stir in it the brussels sprouts with garlic, oil, lemon pepper, and salt.
3. Transfer the mixture to a roasting pan and spread it in an even layer.
4. Bake it for 22 to 26 min. Serve it warm with cheese.
5. Enjoy.

Bubby's
Brussels Sprouts

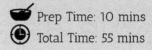

Prep Time: 10 mins
Total Time: 55 mins

Servings per Recipe: 6
Calories	73.3
Fat	3.1g
Cholesterol	6.6mg
Sodium	608.5mg
Carbohydrates	9.7g
Protein	2.4g

Ingredients
3 C. Brussels sprouts, halved
2 green onions, chopped
8 soda crackers, crumbled
1/2 tsp salt
1/4 tsp pepper
1 (10 oz.) can cream of celery soup
1/4 C. milk

Directions
1. Before you do anything, preheat the oven to 325 F.
2. Get a mixing bowl: Mix in it the onions with crackers, soup, milk, a pinch of salt and pepper.
3. Stir in the brussels sprouts and pour the mixture into a baking dish.
4. Bake them for 32 min. Serve them hot.
5. Enjoy.

ROAST BALSAMIC
Apple Brussels Sprouts

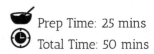

Prep Time: 25 mins
Total Time: 50 mins

Servings per Recipe: 8
Calories	104.2
Fat	5.4g
Cholesterol	0.0mg
Sodium	156.7mg
Carbohydrates	14.1g
Protein	1.5g

Ingredients
12 oz. Brussels sprouts, trimmed and halved
2 sweet cooking apples, cored and cut into wedges
1 C. sliced red onion
3 oz. chopped turkey bacon
3 tbsp olive oil
1/2 tsp salt
1/2 tsp mustard seeds
1/2 tsp ground black pepper

2 tbsp balsamic vinegar
1 tbsp honey
2 tsp Dijon-style mustard

Directions
1. Before you do anything, preheat the oven to 425 F.
2. Line up a baking dish with foil. Place it aside.
3. Get a large mixing bowl: Stir in it the Brussels sprouts, apples, onion, bacon, oil, salt, mustard seeds, and pepper.
4. Transfer the mixture to the lined up pan. Bake them for 26 to 32 min while stirring them halfway through.
5. Get a mixing bowl: Mix in it the vinegar, honey, and Dijon mustard.
6. Pour the mixture over the brussels sprouts and stir them to coat. Serve them warm.
7. Enjoy.

Brussel Sprouts
in November

Prep Time: 15 mins
Total Time: 40 mins

Servings per Recipe: 4
Calories	152.4
Fat	5.9g
Cholesterol	8.0mg
Sodium	94.0mg
Carbohydrates	23.2g
Protein	3.8g

Ingredients
1 1/2 C. sweet potatoes, peeled, cubed
3/4 lb. Brussels sprout, trimmed and halved
1 tbsp butter
1/2 medium onion, chopped
1 - 2 garlic clove, minced
1/4 C. chicken stock

4 tsp brown sugar
1/4 tsp cinnamon
2 tbsp pecan pieces, toasted

Directions
1. Bring a large salted saucepan of water to a boil.
2. Add to it the potatoes and cook them for 15 to 20 min until they become soft.
3. Drain them and place them aside.
4. Microwave the brussels sprouts for 6 min on high. Drain them and place them aside.
5. Place a large pan over medium heat. Heat in it the butter.
6. cook in it the garlic with onion for 3 min.
7. Stir in the sweet potatoes, brussels sprouts, stock, sugar, cinnamon, and pecans.
8. Cook them for 4 min while stirring. Serve them warm.
9. Enjoy.

BARBARA'S
Vegetable Pot

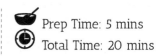
Prep Time: 5 mins
Total Time: 20 mins

Servings per Recipe: 4
Calories	55.9
Fat	3.1g
Cholesterol	7.6mg
Sodium	25.7mg
Carbohydrates	6.7g
Protein	1.5g

Ingredients
1 C. sugar snap pea, trimmed
1 C. Brussels sprout, trimmed and halved
1 orange bell pepper, strips
1 tbsp butter
salt
cracked pepper

Directions
1. Bring a salted pot of water to a boil. Cook in it the brussels sprouts for 8 min.
2. Drain them and place them aside.
3. Bring the same saucepan back to a boil. Cook in it the snap peas for 4 min.
4. Drain them and place them aside.
5. Place a large pan over medium heat. Heat in it the butter.
6. Cook in it the pepper strips for 2 min. Stir in the brussels sprouts with peas, a pinch of salt and pepper.
7. Cook them for 1 min then serve them warm.
8. Enjoy.

Hot
Bunny Sprouts

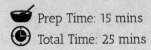 Prep Time: 15 mins

Total Time: 25 mins

Servings per Recipe: 6
Calories   79.8
Fat   4.2g
Cholesterol   10.1mg
Sodium   293.3mg
Carbohydrates   10.2g
Protein   1.7g

Ingredients

1/2 lb. Brussels sprout, trimmed and halved
1 lb. carrot, sliced
2 tbsp butter
1 tbsp orange zest
1 tbsp fresh parsley
1/2 tsp salt

3 drops hot pepper sauce

Directions

1. Place a large deep skillet over medium heat.
2. Stir in it the carrots with brussels sprouts. Cover them with water and put on the lid.
3. Cook them for 12 min until they become tender.
4. Once the time is up, add the butter, zest, parsley, salt, and hot pepper sauce.
5. Stir them to coat then serve them warm.
6. Enjoy.

ITALIAN
Brussels Sprouts

Prep Time: 5 mins
Total Time: 50 mins

Servings per Recipe: 4
Calories   260.6
Fat   20.4g
Cholesterol   0.0mg
Sodium   266.4mg
Carbohydrates   17.8g
Protein   7.0g

Ingredients
2 lbs. Brussels sprouts, trimmed and halved
1 tsp dried thyme
2 tsp dried oregano
1/4 C. pine nuts
1/2 tsp kosher salt
1/4 tsp black pepper
1/4 C. extra-virgin olive oil
1/2 C. balsamic vinegar

Directions
1. Before you do anything, preheat the oven to 425 F.
2. Stir all the ingredients in a roasting pan. Spread them into an even layer.
3. Bake them for 46 min while stirring them halfway through. Serve them warm.
4. Enjoy.

Red Pepper Brussels Sprouts

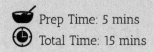

Prep Time: 5 mins
Total Time: 15 mins

Servings per Recipe: 2

Calories	221.6
Fat	15.4g
Cholesterol	20.7mg
Sodium	195.3mg
Carbohydrates	16.9g
Protein	8.3g

Ingredients

1 tbsp olive oil
16 oz. Brussels sprouts, trimmed and sliced
2 tsp crushed red pepper flakes
1/8 C. parmesan cheese
1 tbsp butter
3 tbsp water
salt and pepper

Directions

1. Place a large skillet over medium heat. Heat in it the oil.
2. Cook in it the Brussels sprouts for 3 min.
3. Stir in the red pepper flakes with water, a pinch of salt and pepper. Cook them for 7 to 9 min.
4. Stir in the cheese and serve them warm.
5. Enjoy.

WEEKNIGHT
Brussels Sprouts

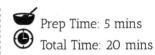

Prep Time: 5 mins
Total Time: 20 mins

Servings per Recipe: 5
Calories	56.8
Fat	3.9g
Cholesterol	9.8mg
Sodium	185.0mg
Carbohydrates	4.4g
Protein	1.8g

Ingredients
3 C. Brussels sprouts
1/2 C. chicken stock
1/4 tsp salt
1/4 tsp pepper
1 1/2 tbsp butter, melted
1/8 tsp caraway seed
1/2 tbsp lemon juice

Directions
1. Place a large saucepan over medium heat. Stir in it the sprouts, stock, salt, and pepper.
2. Put on the lid and cook them until they start boiling.
3. Lower the heat and cook them for 7 to 10 min until they become tender.
4. Get a mixing bowl: Mix in it the butter with lemon juice and caraway seeds.
5. Drizzle the mixture over the brussels sprouts. Serve them warm.
6. Enjoy.

Cream of
Brussels Sprouts

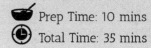 Prep Time: 10 mins
Total Time: 35 mins

Servings per Recipe: 4
Calories   168.7
Fat   13.5g
Cholesterol   22.9mg
Sodium   593.5mg
Carbohydrates   10.1g
Protein   2.4g

Ingredients
1 (16 oz.) bags frozen Brussels sprouts,
cooked
1 (10 3/4 oz.) cans cream of mushroom
soup
1 (8 oz.) containers spreadable cream
cheese with vegetables
3 tbsp butter, melted

3/4 C. crouton

Directions
1. Get a mixing bowl: Mix in it the cream cheese with mushroom soup.
2. Stir in it the brussels sprouts and pour the mixture into a baking pan.
3. Top them with croutons and melted butter.
4. Cook them in the oven for 26 min. Serve them warm.
5. Enjoy.

BRUSSELS SPROUTS
101

Prep Time: 5 mins

Total Time: 20 mins

Servings per Recipe: 4	
Calories	101.8
Fat	11.5g
Cholesterol	30.5mg
Sodium	81.7mg
Carbohydrates	0.0g
Protein	0.1g

Ingredients
Brussels sprout, fresh
4 tbsp butter
allspice, ground
salt
pepper

Directions
1. Bring a large salted pot of water to a boil. Cook in it the brussels sprouts for 7 min.
2. Drain it and place it aside.
3. Place a large pan over medium heat. Heat in it the butter until it melts.
4. Cook in it the brussels sprouts with a pinch of salt and pepper. Cook them for 2 min.
5. Serve them warm with toppings of your choice.
6. Enjoy.

Southern
Spuds and Sprouts

🥣 Prep Time: 10 mins
🕐 Total Time: 23 mins

Servings per Recipe: 5
Calories	150.7
Fat	5.3g
Cholesterol	12.5mg
Sodium	83.0mg
Carbohydrates	23.2g
Protein	4.6g

Ingredients
1 medium onion, chopped
2 tbsp butter
1 large potato, peeled & cubed
1 lb. Brussels sprout
1 bay leaf
1 sweet red pepper, strips
1/4 C. chicken stock

salt and pepper
chopped parsley

Directions
1. Use a sharp knife to make 2 cuts on the bottom of the brussels sprouts.
2. Place a large pan over medium heat. Heat in it the butter.
3. Cook in it the potatoes with onions, and bay leaf for 3 min.
4. Stir in the red pepper and cook them for 3 min.
5. Discard the bay leaf and adjust the seasoning of your brussels sprouts.
6. Garnish them with some parsley.
7. Enjoy.

BRUSSELS SPROUTS
Madrona

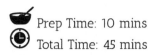

Prep Time: 10 mins
Total Time: 45 mins

Servings per Recipe: 4
Calories	245.2
Fat	16.6g
Cholesterol	0.0mg
Sodium	23.9mg
Carbohydrates	23.5g
Protein	5.7g

Ingredients
4 C. Brussels sprouts, trimmed and halved
2 - 3 C. red seedless grapes
1/2 C. shelled walnuts
2 tbsp olive oil
2 tbsp thyme
kosher salt
ground black pepper
2 - 3 tsp balsamic vinegar

Directions
1. Before you do anything, preheat the oven to 400 F.
2. Combine the brussels sprouts with walnuts on a baking tray.
3. Add to them the olive oil with thyme, a pinch of salt and pepper. Stir them to coat.
4. Spread them in an even layer and bake them for 26 to 32 min.
5. Once the time is up, add the balsamic vinegar and toss them to coat.
6. Serve them warm.
7. Enjoy.

Ballpark
Brussels Sprouts

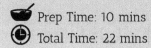

Prep Time: 10 mins
Total Time: 22 mins

Servings per Recipe: 4
Calories   102.7
Fat   7.2g
Cholesterol   0.0mg
Sodium   104.4mg
Carbohydrates   8.4g
Protein   3.3g

Ingredients
4 C. Brussels sprouts, cleaned and cross
cut into the bottom of the stem
1 tbsp margarine
1/2 tsp lemon juice
1/4 C. chopped salted cashews
pepper

Directions
1. Prepare a steamer. Cook in it the brussels sprouts for 8 min.
2. Place a large skillet over medium heat. Heat in it the butter.
3. Stir in the brussels sprouts with lemon juice, a pinch of salt and pepper.
4. Cook them for 2 min. Garnish them with cashews then serve them warm.
5. Enjoy.

HAILEY'S
Favorite

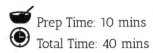 Prep Time: 10 mins

Total Time: 40 mins

Servings per Recipe: 8
Calories   158.0
Fat   11.7g
Cholesterol   7.6mg
Sodium   28.8mg
Carbohydrates   11.8g
Protein   5.1g

Ingredients

1/2 C. hazelnuts, toasted
2 tbsp olive oil
2 tbsp unsalted butter
2 lbs. Brussels sprouts, trimmed and
quartered
kosher salt
2 - 4 tbsp lemon juice
ground black pepper

Directions

1. Prepare a steamer. Cook in it the brussels sprouts for 6 min.
2. Place a large pan over medium heat. Heat in it the oil with butter.
3. Stir in the brussels sprouts with a pinch of salt and pepper. Cook them for 7 min while stirring them often.
4. Stir in 1/4 C. of water and put on half a lid. Cook them for 4 min.
5. Once the time is up, stir in the nuts with lemon juice, a pinch of salt and pepper.
6. Serve them warm.
7. Enjoy.

Brussels Sprouts
with Garlic Mayo

🍲 Prep Time: 15 mins
🕐 Total Time: 30 mins

Servings per Recipe: 5
Calories   171.3
Fat   14.4g
Cholesterol   4.5mg
Sodium   143.6mg
Carbohydrates   10.3g
Protein   2.3g

Ingredients
20 Brussels sprouts, cut into wedges
3 - 4 tbsp olive oil
salt & pepper
Garlic Mayo
6 tbsp mayonnaise
1/4 tsp garlic, minced
1 tsp lemon juice

1 tbsp flat leaf parsley, chopped

Directions
1. To prepare the brussels sprouts:
2. Before you do anything, preheat the oven to 400 F.
3. Toss the brussels sprouts with olive oil, a pinch of salt and pepper in a baking tray.
4. Bake them for 16 min.
5. To prepare the aioli:
6. Get a mixing bowl: Whisk in it the mayonnaise, garlic, parsley and lemon juice.
7. Serve your roasted brussels sprouts with the mayo aioli then serve them warm.
8. Enjoy.

30-MINUTE
Brussels Sprouts

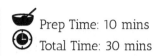

Prep Time: 10 mins
Total Time: 30 mins

Servings per Recipe: 4
Calories   371.3
Fat   27.3g
Cholesterol   7.6mg
Sodium   930.1mg
Carbohydrates   26.3g
Protein   13.5g

Ingredients
2 lbs. Brussels sprouts, trimmed and halved
3 tbsp extra virgin olive oil
1 tbsp unsalted butter
1 C. slivered almonds
2 - 3 tsp kosher salt
2 - 3 tsp black pepper

Directions
1. Place a large pan over high heat. Heat in it the oil.
2. Stir in it the brussels sprouts with a pinch of salt and pepper. Cook them for 6 min.
3. Add the butter and stir them until it melts. Cook them for another 6 min while flipping them.
4. Once the time is up, stir in the almonds. Cook them for an extra 4 min then serve them warm.
5. Enjoy.

Colorado "Slaw"

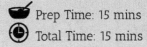 Prep Time: 15 mins
🕐 Total Time: 15 mins

Servings per Recipe: 6
Calories   249.6
Fat   22.3g
Cholesterol   0.0mg
Sodium   24.4mg
Carbohydrates   11.2g
Protein   5.8g

Ingredients
1 1/2 lbs. Brussels sprouts, trimmed and sliced into strips
1 C. walnuts, toasted and crushed
2 tbsp grated pecorino romano cheese
1/4 C. olive oil
3 tbsp lemon juice
ground black pepper

Directions
1. Get a large mixing bowl: Combine in it all the ingredients and stir them to coat.
2. Adjust the seasoning of your salad then serve it.
3. Enjoy.

TAMPA
Vegetable Bowls

Prep Time: 10 mins
Total Time: 40 mins

Servings per Recipe: 4	
Calories	147.8
Fat	7.9g
Cholesterol	0.0mg
Sodium	140.6mg
Carbohydrates	17.4g
Protein	6.4g

Ingredients
1 1/2 lbs. Brussels sprouts, trimmed
4 C. cauliflower
2 tbsp olive oil
1/8 tsp salt
1/8 tsp black pepper

Directions
1. Before you do anything, preheat the oven to 400 F.
2. Get a large mixing bowl: Stir in it the Brussels sprouts and cauliflower with olive oil, salt, and pepper.
3. Pour the mixture into a baking tray and spread it into an even layer.
4. Bake it for 32 min then serve it right away.
5. Enjoy.

4-Ingredient
"Tasty Brussels Sprouts"

🥣 Prep Time: 25 mins
🕐 Total Time: 48 mins

Servings per Recipe: 12
Calories	40.9
Fat	0.5g
Cholesterol	0.0mg
Sodium	23.9mg
Carbohydrates	8.0g
Protein	2.9g

Ingredients
3 lbs. Brussels sprouts, trimmed and halved
1/4 C. dill, chopped
2 tbsp apple cider vinegar
salt & pepper

Directions
1. Bring a large salted pot of water to a boil. Cook in it the brussels sprouts for 7 min.
2. Drain them and transfer them to an ice cold bowl of water. Drain them and transfer them to a baking tray.
3. Add the dill, vinegar, and salt and pepper. Toss them to coat and bake them for 9 min with the lid.
4. Bake them for an extra 6 min uncovered. Serve them warm.
5. Enjoy.

BUTTERED
Brussels Sprouts

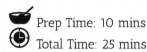

Prep Time: 10 mins
Total Time: 25 mins

Servings per Recipe: 4
Calories	123.4
Fat	11.8g
Cholesterol	30.5mg
Sodium	382.7mg
Carbohydrates	6.1g
Protein	1.6g

Ingredients
1 pint Brussels sprout, halved, outer leaves
removed, bottoms trimmed
1/4 C. butter
1/2 tsp salt
1 lemon, grated for the rind, halved

Directions
1. Prepare a steamer. Cook in it the brussels sprouts for 12 min.
2. Place a large pan over medium heat. Heat in it the butter.
3. Stir in it the brussels sprouts with a pinch of salt and pepper. Cook them for 2 min.
4. Stir in the lemon juice and zest. Cook them for another minute then serve them warm.
5. Enjoy.

Creamy
Parisian Sprouts

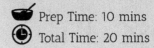 Prep Time: 10 mins
🕐 Total Time: 20 mins

Servings per Recipe: 1
Calories	106.6
Fat	11.0g
Cholesterol	40.7mg
Sodium	302.9mg
Carbohydrates	1.6g
Protein	0.9g

Ingredients
2 (10 oz.) packages frozen Brussels sprouts
3/4 C. heavy cream
3/4 tsp salt
1/8 tsp pepper
1 lemon, zest

Directions
1. Bring a large salted saucepan of water to a boil.
2. Cook in it the brussels sprouts for 6 min. Drain them and place them aside.
3. Place a large saucepan over medium heat, Stir in it the heavy cream, salt, and pepper.
4. Heat them until they start simmering. Keep cooking them until the cream reduces by 1/2 C.
5. Stir in the brussels sprouts with lemon zest. Cook them for 2 to 3 min then serve them warm.
6. Enjoy.

BRUSSELS SPROUTS
Toscano

Prep Time: 10 mins
Total Time: 20 mins

Servings per Recipe: 4
Calories   93.7
Fat   4.5g
Cholesterol   2.2mg
Sodium   108.8mg
Carbohydrates   11.0g
Protein   5.0g

Ingredients
1 lb. Brussels sprout, trimmed
1 tbsp Dijon mustard
2 tsp lemon juice
2 tsp balsamic vinegar
1 tbsp extra virgin olive oil
1 garlic clove, minced
2 tbsp shaved parmesan cheese
1 tsp chopped basil
salt and pepper

Directions
1. Prepare a steamer. Cook in it the brussels sprouts for 11 min.
2. Get a large mixing bowl: Mix in it the mustard with lemon juice, vinegar, oil, garlic, cheese, basil, a pinch of salt and pepper.
3. Add the brussels sprouts and stir them to coat. Serve them immediately.
4. Enjoy.

Prince Edward
Brussels Sprouts

🥣 Prep Time: 10 mins
🕐 Total Time: 40 mins

Servings per Recipe: 4
Calories   132.3
Fat   4.2g
Cholesterol   0.0mg
Sodium   38.4mg
Carbohydrates   22.2g
Protein   4.7g

Ingredients

1 tbsp vegetable oil
1 large onion, halved and sliced
1 1/2 lbs. Brussels sprouts, halved
2 tbsp maple syrup
1 dash salt and pepper

Directions

1. Place a large pan over medium heat. Heat in it the oil.
2. Sauté in it the onions for 22 min while stirring them often.
3. Stir in the brussels sprouts with 1/4 C. of water. Turn up the heat and put on the lid.
4. Cook them for 6 min. Add the maple syrup and cook them 8 to 12 min.
5. Adjust the seasoning of your brussels sprouts skillets then serve it warm.
6. Enjoy.

HOW TO FRY
Brussels Sprouts

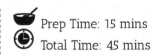 Prep Time: 15 mins
Total Time: 45 mins

Servings per Recipe: 4
Calories	567.6
Fat	22.9g
Cholesterol	256.1mg
Sodium	1918.2mg
Carbohydrates	53.6g
Protein	37.8g

Ingredients
1 -1 1/2 lb. Brussels sprout, halved
2 C. seasoned breadcrumbs
2 C. grated parmesan cheese
salt and pepper
Italian spices
4 eggs

Directions
1. Trim and make two cuts in the shape of an X on the bottom of each brussels sprout.
2. Place a large salted pot of water to a boil. Heat it until it starts boiling.
3. Cook in it the brussels sprouts for 7 min. Drain them and place them in an ice cold bowl of water.
4. Drain them and place them aside.
5. Get a mixing bowl: Mix in it the bread crumbs, parmesan cheese, and seasonings.
6. Get a mixing bowl: Whisk in it the eggs.
7. Place a large pan over medium heat. Heat in it the oil.
8. Dip a brussels sprout in the beaten egg and coat it with the breadcrumbs mixture.
9. Repeat the process with the remaining brussels sprouts and fry them in batches until they become golden brown.
10. Serve them warm with toppings of your choice.
11. Enjoy.

Asian Fusion
Brussels Sprouts

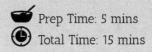

Prep Time: 5 mins
Total Time: 15 mins

Servings per Recipe: 2
Calories	62.2
Fat	0.7g
Cholesterol	0.0mg
Sodium	332.9mg
Carbohydrates	12.2g
Protein	4.3g

Ingredients
10 oz. Brussels sprouts, trimmed
1 C. water
1 tbsp low sodium soy sauce
2 tbsp minced ginger
2 minced garlic cloves
1/2-1 tbsp Splenda granular
1/8 tbsp red pepper flakes

Directions
1. Place a large saucepan over medium heat.
2. Stir in it all the ingredients and cook them until they start boiling.
3. Lower the heat and let them cook for 10 to 12 min. Serve it warm.
4. Enjoy.

BRUSSEL SPROUT
and Cabbage Stir Fry

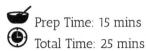

Prep Time: 15 mins
Total Time: 25 mins

Servings per Recipe: 4
Calories	135.7
Fat	6.5g
Cholesterol	15.2mg
Sodium	1847.1mg
Carbohydrates	18.5g
Protein	4.9g

Ingredients
1 lb. Brussels sprout, trimmed and halved
1 tbsp salt
2 tbsp butter, unsalted
1 small red cabbage, cored and sliced
kosher salt
black pepper, ground

Directions
1. Bring a large saucepan of water to a boil. Stir into it 1 tbsp of salt.
2. Cook in it the brussels sprouts for 2 min. Drain them and transfer them to an ice cold bowl of water.
3. Drain them and pat them dry.
4. Place a large pan over medium heat. Heat in it the butter.
5. Cook in it the brussels sprouts for 2 min. Stir in the cabbage with a pinch of salt and pepper.
6. Cook them for 3 min then serve them warm.
7. Enjoy.

Brussels Sprouts
Plates

Prep Time: 10 mins
Total Time: 20 mins

Servings per Recipe: 4
Calories   206.5
Fat   14.2g
Cholesterol   0.0mg
Sodium   318.8mg
Carbohydrates   18.4g
Protein   4.7g

Ingredients

20 Brussels sprouts, trimmed and halved lengthwise
1/4 C. olive oil
1 tbsp vinegar
1/2 tbsp balsamic vinegar
2 garlic, minced
1 tbsp black pepper, grounded

1/2 tbsp salt

Directions

1. Prepare a steamer. Cook in it the brussels sprouts for 9 min.
2. Get a large mixing bowl: Whisk in it the oil with vinegar, garlic, salt, and pepper.
3. Add the brussels sprouts and toss them to coat. Serve them immediately.
4. Enjoy.

SIMPLE SESAME
Brussels Sprouts

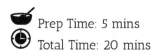

Prep Time: 5 mins
Total Time: 20 mins

Servings per Recipe: 4
Calories   112.5
Fat   8.5g
Cholesterol   7.6mg
Sodium   50.2mg
Carbohydrates   8.2g
Protein   3.0g

Ingredients
1 tbsp butter
1 1/2 tbsp sesame oil
2 tbsp parsley, chopped
2 tbsp chives, chopped
1 lb. Brussels sprout, trimmed
salt
pepper

Directions
1. Get a mixing bowl: Mix in it the butter, sesame oil, parsley, and chives.
2. Place a large salted pot of water over high heat. Bring it to a boil.
3. Cook in it the brussels sprouts for 11 min. Drain them and transfer them to a skillet.
4. Cook them for 1 min. Add the butter with a pinch of salt and pepper.
5. Stir them to coat then serve them warm.
6. Enjoy.

Lindsey's Kitchen
Brussels Sprouts

🥣 Prep Time: 10 mins
🕐 Total Time: 15 mins

Servings per Recipe: 3
Calories	29.9
Fat	0.3g
Cholesterol	0.0mg
Sodium	12.0mg
Carbohydrates	6.2g
Protein	1.6g

Ingredients
2 C. Brussels sprouts, quartered
2 minced garlic cloves
1/2 inch piece ginger, peeled and sliced
1/2 onion, sliced thin
1/2 tbsp red pepper flakes
soy sauce
cornstarch

sugar
sesame oil

Directions
1. Place a large pan over medium heat. Heat in it the oil.
2. Add the brussels sprouts with onion, garlic, and ginger. Cook them for 3 min.
3. Get a mixing bowl: Mix in it 1 tbsp of soy sauce, 1 tsp of sugar, 1 tsp of cornstarch and 1 tbsp of sesame oil.
4. Stir in the crushed red pepper with the oil mixture, a pinch of salt and pepper.
5. Cook them for 2 to 3 min then serve them warm.
6. Enjoy.

FRENCH
Brussels Sprouts Gratin

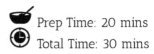 Prep Time: 20 mins

Total Time: 30 mins

Servings per Recipe: 6
Calories	258.6
Fat	18.5g
Cholesterol	47.8mg
Sodium	316.0mg
Carbohydrates	14.8g
Protein	11.1g

Ingredients
1 1/2 lbs. Brussels sprouts, trim and rinse
1 1/2 tbsp butter
1/4 tbsp salt
2 tbsp flour
1/4 C. milk, plus
2 tbsp milk
1 C. sour cream
2 tbsp grated parmesan cheese
1 C. shredded cheddar cheese

Directions
1. Bring a large salted pot of water to a boil.
2. Cook in it the brussels sprouts for 7 min. Drain it and transfer to a baking dish.
3. Place a heavy saucepan over medium heat. Stir in it the butter until it melts.
4. Mix in the flour with a pinch of salt for 1 min.
5. Turn off the heat and add the milk with sour cream while whisking until no lumps are found.
6. Place the sauce back on the heat and cook it until it becomes thick while stirring.
7. Add the parmesan cheese and stir it until it melts.
8. Pour the sauce over the brussels sprouts and top it with cheddar cheese.
9. Before you do anything, preheat the oven broiler.
10. Bake it for 5 to 6 min until the cheese melts. Serve it hot.
11. Enjoy.

Gilroy
Garlic Festival Brussels Sprouts

Prep Time: 10 mins
Total Time: 30 mins

Servings per Recipe: 2
Calories   263.0
Fat   23.7g
Cholesterol   61.0mg
Sodium   195.0mg
Carbohydrates   11.9g
Protein   4.2g

Ingredients
14 - 40 Brussels sprouts, trimmed
1/4 C. butter, melted
3 cloves garlic, minced
salt
pepper

Directions
1. Use a shape knife to make to cuts in the shape of X on the bottom of each brussel sprout.
2. Prepare a steamer. Cook in it the brussels sprouts for 22 min.
3. Place a large skillet over medium heat. Heat in it the butter. Cook in it the garlic for 3 min.
4. Add the brussels sprouts with a pinch of salt and pepper. Cook them for 1 min then serve them warm.
5. Enjoy.

SWEET PEPPERY
Brussels

Prep Time: 10 mins
Total Time: 25 mins

Servings per Recipe: 3
Calories	136.7
Fat	10.3g
Cholesterol	2.9mg
Sodium	452.2mg
Carbohydrates	8.8g
Protein	2.8g

Ingredients
1 pint Brussels sprouts, cooked
2 tbsp cooking oil
1/4 C. cider vinegar
1 tbsp sugar
1/2 tbsp salt
1/4 tbsp pepper
2 tbsp grated parmesan cheese

Directions
1. Before you do anything, preheat the oven to 350 F.
2. Get a mixing bowl: Whisk in it the oil, vinegar, sugar, salt, and pepper.
3. Add the brussels sprouts and stir them to coat. Pour the mixture into a baking dish.
4. Top it with cheese then bake it for 16 min. Serve it warm.
5. Enjoy.

Mushrooms and Sprouts

Prep Time: 30 mins
Total Time: 45 mins

Servings per Recipe: 1
Calories   154.0
Fat   11.5g
Cholesterol   0.0mg
Sodium   483.3mg
Carbohydrates   12.3g
Protein   3.9g

Ingredients

3/4 lb. small Brussels sprout, trimmed
1 lb. small mushroom
1/4 C. olive oil
1/2 C. lemon juice
1 C. water
1 tbsp salt
1/4 tbsp ground black pepper

2 cloves garlic, halved
1 bay leaf
1/2 tbsp oregano
1/2 tbsp basil
1/2 tbsp thyme
1 tbsp chopped parsley

Directions

1. Bring a large salted pot of water to a boil. Cook in it the brussels sprouts for 7 min.
2. Drain them and transfer them to a large mixing bowl.
3. Place a saucepan over medium heat. Combine in it the oil with lemon juice, water, garlic, bay leaf, herbs, salt, and pepper.
4. Heat them until they start boiling. Turn off the heat and let it lose heat for a while.
5. Add it to the brussels sprouts with mushrooms. Let them sit in the fridge for at least 3 h.
6. Once the time is up, drain them and serve them cold.
7. Enjoy.

PERSIAN
Brussels Sprouts

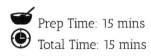

Prep Time: 15 mins
Total Time: 15 mins

Servings per Recipe: 3
Calories	70.8
Fat	5.0g
Cholesterol	0.0mg
Sodium	12.1mg
Carbohydrates	5.8g
Protein	2.6g

Ingredients

1/2 lb. Brussels sprout, quartered
salt and pepper
1 lemon, zest
2 - 3 tbsp pomegranate molasses
1/4 C. toasted walnuts, chopped
1 lemon, juice
4 tbsp extra virgin olive oil

Directions

1. Bring a large saucepan of water with 1 tsp of salt to a boil.
2. Cook in it the brussels sprouts for 4 to 5 min. Drain it and place it aside.
3. Get a large mixing bowl: Whisk in it the lemon zest with olive oil, molasses, lemon juice, and oil.
4. Add the walnuts with brussels sprouts. Stir them to coat.
5. Chill the salad in the fridge until ready to serve.
6. Enjoy.

Missouri
Brussel Sprouts Casserole

🥣 Prep Time: 10 mins
🕐 Total Time: 40 mins

Servings per Recipe: 6
Calories	154.5
Fat	8.1g
Cholesterol	20.9mg
Sodium	138.8mg
Carbohydrates	17.2g
Protein	5.4g

Ingredients
3 tbsp butter
2 celery ribs, chopped
1 onion, chopped
1 1/2 lbs. Brussels sprouts, small and trimmed
2 tbsp flour
1 C. milk, heated

salt
ground pepper
allspice, ground
1/4 C. dry breadcrumbs

Directions
1. Before you do anything, preheat the oven to 350 F.
2. Prepare a steamer. Cook in it the brussels sprouts for 7 min.
3. Place a large pan over medium heat. Heat in it 2 tbsp of butter.
4. Cook in it the onion with celery for 9 min. Add the flour and mix them well.
5. Add the milk gradually while whisking.
6. Stir in the brussels sprouts with allspice, a pinch of salt and pepper. Stir them to coat.
7. Transfer the mixture to a baking dish. Sprinkle over it the bread crumbs and butter.
8. Cook it in the oven for 10 to 12 min. Serve it warm.
9. Enjoy.

ENCHANTED FOREST
Brussels Sprouts

🍳 Prep Time: 10 mins
🕐 Total Time: 55 mins

Servings per Recipe: 4
Calories   130.3
Fat   6.4g
Cholesterol   4.8mg
Sodium   800.4mg
Carbohydrates   13.5g
Protein   8.2g

Ingredients
30 Brussels sprouts, trimmed and quartered
olive oil
1 1/2 tbsp kosher salt
1/2-1 tbsp -cracked black pepper
1/2 tbsp garlic powder
1/3 C. sliced almonds
1/3 C. grated Parmigiano-Reggiano cheese
1 1/2 tbsp white truffle oil

Directions
1. Before you do anything, preheat the oven to 400 F.
2. Place the Brussels sprouts and almonds on a baking tray.
3. Pour over them the olive oil. Add the garlic powder with a pinch of salt and pepper.
4. Stir them to coat and spread them in the pan. Bake them for 36 min.
5. Stir them and top them with cheese. Bake them for 9 to 10 min. Serve them warm with a drizzle of truffle oil.
6. Enjoy.

Cheddar
Sprouts

Prep Time: 10 mins
Total Time: 30 mins

Servings per Recipe: 4
Calories   594.9
Fat   40.7g
Cholesterol   81.1mg
Sodium   535.4mg
Carbohydrates   37.9g
Protein   23.8g

Ingredients

2 lbs. Brussels sprouts, cleaned and trimmed
4 tbsp olive oil
salt & ground black pepper
2 tbsp butter
3 tbsp flour
2 1/2 C. milk

1 1/2 C. sharp cheddar cheese, grated
1/2 C. breadcrumbs
salt & ground black pepper

Directions

1. Before you do anything, preheat the oven to 400 F.
2. Stir the brussels sprouts with oil, a pinch of salt and pepper in a baking sheet.
3. Bake them for 32 to 42 min.
4. Place a large pan over medium heat. Heat in it the butter.
5. Add the flour and mix them well. Add the milk gradually while whisking until no lumps are found.
6. Lower the heat and cook the sauce for 3 min.
7. Turn off the heat then add the cheese with a pinch of salt and pepper. Stir it until it melts.
8. Grease a baking dish with some butter and sprinkle in it some breadcrumbs.
9. Arrange over it the brussels sprouts and top them with the cheese sauce.
10. Sprinkle the remaining cheese and breadcrumbs on top. Bake it for 16 to 22 min.
11. Serve your brussels sprouts casserole hot.
12. Enjoy.

GRAPES
and Brussels Sprouts

Prep Time: 10 mins
Total Time: 15 mins

Servings per Recipe: 4
Calories   137.3
Fat   8.6g
Cholesterol   15.2mg
Sodium   66.7mg
Carbohydrates   12.7g
Protein   4.0g

Ingredients
1 lb. baby Brussels sprout
2 tbsp butter
1/2 C. green seedless grape
2 tbsp broth, optional
2 tbsp blanched slivered almonds

Directions
1. Bring a large salted pot of water to a boil. Cook in it the brussels sprouts for 9 min.
2. Drain it and place it aside.
3. Place a large pan over medium heat. Heat in it the butter.
4. Cook in it the brussels sprouts for 4 min.
5. Stir in the broth with almonds and grapes. Heat them for 1 min then serve them warm.
6. Enjoy

Sweet Leeks
and Brussels Sprouts

🥣 Prep Time: 10 mins
🕐 Total Time: 40 mins

Servings per Recipe: 8
Calories   123.3
Fat   5.4g
Cholesterol   0.0mg
Sodium   29.5mg
Carbohydrates   18.1g
Protein   3.8g

Ingredients

1 large leek, trimmed and julienned
3 tbsp olive oil, divided
30 oz. Brussels sprouts, trimmed and
halved
1/3 C. dried cranberries
3 tbsp honey
3 tbsp walnuts

Directions

1. Before you do anything, preheat the oven to 400 F.
2. Stir the leeks with 1 1 tbsp of oil in a baking tray.
3. surround it with the brussels sprouts then season them with a pinch of salt and pepper.
4. Bake them for 22 min.
5. Transfer them to a mixing bowl and add to them the remaining ingredients.
6. Stir them to coat and serve them right away.
7. Enjoy.

GARDEN
Brussels Sprouts

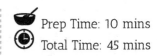

Prep Time: 10 mins
Total Time: 45 mins

Servings per Recipe: 6
Calories	149.2
Fat	11.5g
Cholesterol	0.0mg
Sodium	95.3mg
Carbohydrates	10.4g
Protein	2.8g

Ingredients
1 (16 oz.) packages fresh Brussels sprouts
1 small red onion, sliced
5 tbsp olive oil, divided
1/4 tbsp kosher salt
1/4 tbsp ground black pepper
1 shallot, chopped
4 tbsp balsamic vinegar
1 tbsp chopped rosemary

Directions
1. Before you do anything, preheat the oven to 425 F.
2. Get a large mixing bowl: Mix in it the onion with brussels sprouts, 3 tbsp of olive oil, a pinch of salt and pepper.
3. Transfer the mixture to a baking tray and bake them for 26 to 32 min.
4. Place a large pan over medium heat. Heat in it the remaining oil.
5. Cook in it the shallot for 5 to 6 min.
6. Stir in the balsamic vinegar and cook them for 4 min.
7. Stir in the rosemary and add them to the brussels sprouts mixture. Stir them to coat and serve them.
8. Enjoy.

Brussels Sprouts
Ontario

🥣 Prep Time: 5 mins
🕐 Total Time: 15 mins

Servings per Recipe: 2
Calories   63.7
Fat   2.6g
Cholesterol   0.0mg
Sodium   615.9mg
Carbohydrates   9.6g
Protein   1.8g

Ingredients
6 Brussels sprouts, trimmed and halved
1/2 tbsp salt
1 carrot
1 tbsp olive oil
1 tbsp pure maple syrup
salt and pepper

Directions
1. Bring a large salted pot of water to a boil. Cook in it the brussels sprouts for 4 min.
2. Drain it and place it aside. Stir the carrots into the same pot and cook them for 4 min.
3. Drain them and place them aside.
4. Place a large pan over medium heat. Heat in it the oil.
5. Cook in it the carrots with brussels sprouts for 3 min.
6. Stir in the maple syrup with a pinch of salt and pepper. Serve them warm.
7. Enjoy.

BALSAMIC
Apple Brussels Sprouts

🥣 Prep Time: 4 mins
🕐 Total Time: 19 mins

Servings per Recipe: 2
Calories   256.4
Fat   13.8g
Cholesterol   10.2mg
Sodium   39.2mg
Carbohydrates   31.4g
Protein   5.5g

Ingredients
10 oz. Brussels sprouts stem removed and halved
1 tbsp olive oil
kosher salt
pepper
3 tbsp balsamic vinegar
1 tbsp honey
2 tbsp pistachios, toasted and chopped
1/2 fuji apple, unpeeled and sliced

1 tbsp crème fraiche

Directions
1. Before you do anything, preheat the oven to 450 F.

2. Stir the brussels sprouts with olive oil, a pinch of salt and pepper on a baking tray.

3. Bake them for 18 min.

4. Place a large skillet over medium heat. Stir in it the honey with balsamic vinegar. cook them for 4 min.

5. Get a large mixing bowl: Toss in it the brussels sprouts with vinegar sauce, apple slices, and pistachios.

6. Serve it with some crème fraiche.

7. Enjoy.

Brussels Sprouts
Salad

🥣 Prep Time: 10 mins
🕐 Total Time: 30 mins

Servings per Recipe: 4
Calories   160.4
Fat   11.7g
Cholesterol   3.8mg
Sodium   40.2mg
Carbohydrates   12.6g
Protein   5.1g

Ingredients

1/3 C. pecans, toasted and chopped
2 (10 oz.) containers Brussels sprouts, ends trimmed
1/2 tbsp butter
2 tbsp olive oil
1 tbsp yellow mustard seeds
1 - 2 tbsp lemon juice

salt and pepper

Directions

1. Get a food processor: Place it in the brussels sprouts and pulse them several times until they become shredded.
2. Place a large pan over medium heat. Heat in it the butter with oil.
3. Toast in it the mustard seeds for 40 sec.
4. Stir in the shredded brussels sprouts. Cook them for 8 min.
5. Add the lemon juice with a pinch of salt and pepper. Stir them to coat then serve them warm.
6. Enjoy.

BRUSSELS SPROUTS
in a Firehouse

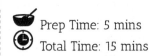

Prep Time: 5 mins
Total Time: 15 mins

Servings per Recipe: 6
Calories	99.5
Fat	2.9g
Cholesterol	34.0mg
Sodium	167.0mg
Carbohydrates	13.8g
Protein	5.1g

Ingredients
4 C. cooked Brussels sprouts
1 egg, beaten
3/4 C. dry breadcrumbs
1 tbsp Italian seasoning
oil
1/4 C. cheese

Directions
1. Get a mixing bowl: Combine in it the bread crumbs with Italian seasoning.
2. Place a large pan over medium-high heat. Heat in it 1 inch of oil.
3. Coat the brussels sprouts with the beaten egg then roll them in the breadcrumbs mixture.
4. Deep fry them until they become golden brown. Serve them warm.
5. Enjoy.

Stir Fried
Brussels Sprouts with Bacon

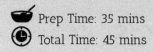

Prep Time: 35 mins
Total Time: 45 mins

Servings per Recipe: 8
Calories	87.7
Fat	4.6g
Cholesterol	2.7mg
Sodium	92.1mg
Carbohydrates	9.2g
Protein	4.5g

Ingredients
2 lbs. Brussels sprouts, sliced
1 tbsp vegetable oil
8 oz. turkey bacon, strips
salt
ground black pepper
crushed red pepper flakes
3 - 4 tbsp toasted & chopped cashews

1/4 C. grated parmesan cheese

Directions
1. Place a large saucepan over high heat. Heat in it the oil.
2. Cook in it the turkey bacon for 6 min. Lower the heat and stir in the brussels sprouts. Cook them for 4 min.
3. Stir in the cashews with red pepper flakes, a pinch of salt and pepper.
4. Add the cheese and stir it until it melts. Serve it warm.
5. Enjoy.

BRUSSEL SPROUT
Masala

Prep Time: 3 mins
Total Time: 10 mins

Servings per Recipe: 6
Calories   134.7
Fat   9.8g
Cholesterol   0.0mg
Sodium   419.3mg
Carbohydrates   10.7g
Protein   3.8g

Ingredients
2 lbs. Brussels sprouts, thawed or cooked
and cooled
1/4 C. vegetable oil
1 tbsp salt
1 tbsp garam masala powder

Directions
1. Place a large pan over medium heat. Heat in it the oil.
2. Cook in it the Brussels sprouts until they become golden.
3. Stir in 3 tbsp of water with curry powder and a pinch of salt.
4. Cook them for an extra 6 min until they become tender. Serve them warm.
5. Enjoy.

Real Mediterranean
Brussel Sprouts

Prep Time: 10 mins
Total Time: 30 mins

Servings per Recipe: 2
Calories   176.5
Fat   8.6g
Cholesterol   15.2mg
Sodium   111.9mg
Carbohydrates   22.2g
Protein   8.7g

Ingredients

1 lb. Brussels sprout, trimmed
1 tbsp butter, melted
1 tbsp lemon juice
1/2 tbsp dill weed
1 tbsp lemon zest
salt
pepper

1 tbsp almonds, chopped

Directions

1. Use a sharp knife to cut 2 slices in the bottom of each brussels sprout in the shape of X.
2. Bring a large salted pot of water to a boil. Stir into it the brussels sprouts.
3. Put on the lid and lower the heat. Cook them for 10 min.
4. Place a skillet over medium heat. Heat in it the butter until it melts.
5. Stir in the lemon juice with dill weed, and lemon zest. Add the brussels sprouts and stir them for 1 min.
6. Stir in the almonds then serve them warm.
7. Enjoy.

RESTAURANT
Brussel Sprouts

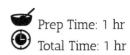

Prep Time: 1 hr
Total Time: 1 hr

Servings per Recipe: 8
Calories	190.6
Fat	12.9g
Cholesterol	7.7mg
Sodium	83.2mg
Carbohydrates	17.2g
Protein	5.2g

Ingredients
1 C. walnuts, toasted and chopped
1 lb. Brussels sprout, trimmed and halved
1 pint small shallots
2 tbsp unsalted butter, divided
1 tbsp sugar
salt and pepper
1 fennel bulb, julienned
1/2 C. vegetable broth

Directions
1. Bring a large salted pot of water to a boil. Cook in it the brussels sprouts for 9 min.
2. Drain it and place it aside.
3. Cook the shallots in the same pot for 2 to 3 min. Drain them and peel them.
4. Place a large pan over medium heat. Heat in it 1 tbsp of butter.
5. Stir in it the shallots with sugar, a pinch of salt and pepper. Put on the lid and cook them for 8 min.
6. Stir in the fennel and cook them for extra 6 min.
7. Place a small saucepan over medium heat. Combine in it the broth with walnuts.
8. Heat them until they start boiling. Lower the heat and keep it boiling the sauce becomes thick.
9. Stir it into the shallot mixture with 1 tbsp of butter and brussels sprouts.
10. Serve them warm with some rice.
11. Enjoy.

Oniony
Sprouts

🥣 Prep Time: 40 mins
🕐 Total Time: 40 mins

Servings per Recipe: 6
Calories   246.1
Fat   16.9g
Cholesterol   40.6mg
Sodium   412.1mg
Carbohydrates   20.3g
Protein   7.9g

Ingredients

3 - 4 lbs. Brussels sprouts
2 medium chopped onions
2 C. chicken broth
1 tbsp lemon juice
1/2 C. butter
salt and pepper

Directions

1. Place a skillet over medium heat. Heat in it the butter.
2. Cook in it the onion for 4 min. Stir in the lemon juice with a pinch of salt. Turn off the heat.
3. Place a large saucepan over high heat. Heat in it the broth until it starts boiling.
4. Cook in it the brussels sprouts for 9 min. Drain it and place it aside.
5. Stir the remaining broth into the onion pan and cook them until it evaporates.
6. Add the brussels sprouts and stir them then serve them warm.
7. Enjoy.

WONDA'S
Award Winning Quiche

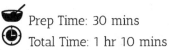

Prep Time: 30 mins

Total Time: 1 hr 10 mins

Servings per Recipe: 8

Calories	377.3
Fat	25.0g
Cholesterol	190.9mg
Sodium	427.1mg
Carbohydrates	26.4g
Protein	13.2g

Ingredients
1 tbsp butter
1/2 C. vegetable stock
2 leeks, washed and chopped
1 large onion, diced
30 Brussels sprouts, peeled and quartered
2 garlic cloves, minced
1 spring onion, sliced
1 tbsp herbs de Provence
5 oz. Philadelphia Cream Cheese

1 C. cheese, grated
1/2 C. cream
6 eggs, beaten
salt
pepper
1 (30 cm) unbaked pie shells

Directions
1. Place a large skillet over medium heat.
2. Combine in it the onion with butter, stock, leeks, brussels sprouts, garlic, spring onion, and herbs de Provence.
3. Cook them for 8 min while stirring them often. Turn off the heat and let them cool down for a while.
4. Stir in the cream cheese with cheese, cream, eggs, a pinch of salt and pepper.
5. Spoon the mixture into the pie shell. Bake it for 42 min.
6. Serve your pie warm.
7. Enjoy.

German Inspired Brussels Sprouts

Prep Time: 3 mins
Total Time: 10 mins

Servings per Recipe: 12
Calories   125.6
Fat   11.6g
Cholesterol   17.6mg
Sodium   207.4mg
Carbohydrates   5.2g
Protein   1.2g

Ingredients

2/3 C. mayonnaise
2/3 C. sour cream
1/4 C. Dijon mustard
1/2 tbsp garlic salt
1 tbsp Worcestershire sauce
1/2 tbsp hot sauce
4 (10 oz.) packages frozen Brussels sprouts

3 tbsp butter, melted
1/4 C. chopped pecans

Directions

1. Place a large skillet over medium heat. Stir in it the mayonnaise, sour cream, mustard, garlic salt, Worcestershire sauce, and hot sauce.
2. Cook it for 3 to 5 min over low heat while stirring it often.
3. Prepare the brussels sprouts by following the instructions on the package.
4. Drain them and add them the pan with butter, and pecans.
5. Season them with a pinch of salt and pepper. Stir them to coat then serve them warm.
6. Enjoy.

WEST VIRGINIA
Vegetable Roast

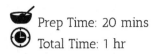 Prep Time: 20 mins
Total Time: 1 hr

Servings per Recipe: 6
Calories	224.4
Fat	12.5g
Cholesterol	0.0mg
Sodium	153.5mg
Carbohydrates	27.0g
Protein	3.3g

Ingredients
1/3 C. extra virgin olive oil
3 medium carrots, cut into circles
1 1/2 C. Brussels sprouts, halved
4 C. Red Bliss potatoes, sliced
3 medium parsnips, sliced
1 C. sweet potato, sliced
1 tbsp dried oregano
1 tbsp dried rosemary
1 tbsp dried thyme

1 tbsp dried basil
1/4 tbsp sea salt
2 tbsp black pepper

Directions
1. Before you do anything, preheat the oven to 400 F.
2. Stir the veggies with herbs, a pinch of salt and pepper in an oil greased baking tray.
3. Add more oil if needed. Bake them for 36 to 42 min. Serve them warm.
4. Enjoy.

Parmesan
Brussels Sprout Bowls

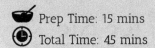 Prep Time: 15 mins

Total Time: 45 mins

Servings per Recipe: 4
Calories   249.3
Fat   15.0g
Cholesterol   0.0mg
Sodium   114.6mg
Carbohydrates   26.5g
Protein   10.1g

Ingredients

2 lbs. broccoli florets, chopped
1 lb. Brussels sprout, trimmed and halved
3 garlic cloves, minced
4 tbsp olive oil, divided
salt and pepper
1 tbsp honey
2 tbsp Dijon mustard

1 lemon, juice and zest
1 pinch cayenne
salt and pepper
1/4-1/2 C. parmesan cheese

Directions

1. Before you do anything, preheat the oven to 425 F.
2. Stir the broccoli with brussels sprouts, garlic, 2 tbsp of olive oil, a pinch of salt and pepper in a baking tray.
3. Bake them for 22 to 32 min while stirring them halfway through.
4. Get a mixing bowl: Mix in it the 2 tbsp oil, honey, lemon juice and zest, Dijon, cayenne and salt, and pepper.
5. Add them to the roasted veggies and toss them to coat. Serve them warm.
6. Enjoy.

SUN DRIED TOMATO
Brussels Sprouts

Prep Time: 10 mins
Total Time: 17 mins

Servings per Recipe: 4

Calories	113.3
Fat	7.9g
Cholesterol	0.0mg
Sodium	36.2mg
Carbohydrates	9.9g
Protein	3.2g

Ingredients
2 tbsp extra virgin olive oil
2 cloves garlic, chopped
1 lb. Brussels sprout, trimmed and sliced
6 pieces sun-dried tomatoes packed in oil, shredded
1 grated lemon, zest
1-2 tbsp lemon juice

Directions
1. Place a large skillet over high heat. Heat in it the oil.
2. Cook in it the garlic for 10 sec. Stir in the brussels sprouts and cook them for 4 to 5 min.
3. Add the dry tomato strips with lemon zest, lemon juice, a pinch of salt and pepper.
4. Toss them to coat then serve them warm.
5. Enjoy.

Almond
Brussels Sprouts

Prep Time: 10 mins
Total Time: 15 mins

Servings per Recipe: 4
Calories   132.2
Fat   8.1g
Cholesterol   7.6mg
Sodium   97.9mg
Carbohydrates   12.5g
Protein   5.3g

Ingredients
1 lb. Brussels sprout, chopped
1/4-1/3 C. raw almonds, chopped
2 - 3 tbsp lemon rind, minced
2 - 4 tbsp plain breadcrumbs
1 tbsp butter
salt
pepper

Directions
1. Place a large saucepan over medium heat. Heat in it the butter until it melts.
2. Cook in it the breadcrumbs with lemon zest, and almonds for 3 min.
3. Place a large skillet over high heat. Stir in it a splash of water with brussels sprouts, oil, a pinch of salt and pepper.
4. Put on the lid and cook them for 6 to 8 min until they become tender while stirring them often.
5. Add the almonds mixture and stir them to coat. Serve them warm.
6. Enjoy.

BRUSSELS SPROUTS
with Dijon Vinaigrette

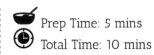

Prep Time: 5 mins
Total Time: 10 mins

Servings per Recipe: 8
Calories   94.8
Fat   6.2g
Cholesterol   15.2mg
Sodium   103.0mg
Carbohydrates   8.2g
Protein   3.6g

Ingredients
1 1/2 lbs. frozen Brussels sprouts
1/4 C. butter
1/2 C. minced red onion
2 tbsp chopped parsley
2 tbsp Dijon mustard
1 tbsp minced garlic
1 1/2 tbsp balsamic vinegar
1 pinch granulated sugar
ground black pepper

Directions
1. Prepare the brussels sprouts by following the instructions on the package.
2. Place a large skillet over medium heat. Heat in it the butter.
3. Stir in it the onion, parsley, mustard, garlic, vinegar, sugar, and pepper.
4. Cook them for 2 to 3 min. Stir in the brussels sprouts.
5. Put on the lid and cook them for 2 to 3 min. Serve them warm.
6. Enjoy.

Brussels Sprouts
with Greek Dressing

Prep Time: 3 mins
Total Time: 10 mins

Servings per Recipe: 4
Calories   147.8
Fat   11.5g
Cholesterol   2.2mg
Sodium   323.7mg
Carbohydrates   9.4g
Protein   4.1g

Ingredients

1 lb. Brussels sprout, trimmed and quartered
Dressing
3 tbsp extra virgin olive oil
2 tbsp lemon juice
2 medium garlic cloves, minced
1 tbsp Dijon mustard

1 tbsp parsley, minced
1/2 tbsp kosher salt
1/4 tbsp black pepper
2 tbsp parmesan cheese, grated
1 tbsp lemon zest, cut into matchstick

Directions

1. Prepare a steamer. Cook in it the brussels sprouts for 9 to 10 min.

2. Get a large mixing bowl: Whisk in it all the dressing ingredients.

3. Add the brussels sprouts and stir them to coat. Serve them immediately.

4. Enjoy.

COUNTRY BAKED
Chicken Thighs

Prep Time: 5 mins
Total Time: 40 mins

Servings per Recipe: 4
Calories	323.3
Fat	24.7g
Cholesterol	78.9mg
Sodium	119.8mg
Carbohydrates	7.9g
Protein	17.5g

Ingredients
4 skin-on chicken thighs
1 1/2 C. Brussels sprouts, halved
4 carrots, cut on the bias
3 tbsp olive oil
1 tbsp Herbs de Provence

Directions
1. Before you do anything, preheat the oven to 400 F.
2. Get a large mixing bowl: Stir in it the veggies with 1½ tbsp olive oil, ½ tsp herbs and salt and pepper.
3. Transfer the mixture to a baking sheet and spread it in an even layer.
4. Get a mixing bowl: Toss in it the chicken thighs with 1½ tbsp olive oil, ½ tsp herbs and salt and pepper.
5. Arrange it next to the veggies on the pan. Bake them for 32 to 36 in. Serve them warm.
6. Enjoy.

Garden

Brussel Sprouts with Pears

🥘 Prep Time: 15 mins
🕐 Total Time: 1 hr

Servings per Recipe: 4
Calories   200.8
Fat   14.2g
Cholesterol   0.0mg
Sodium   348.1mg
Carbohydrates   17.5g
Protein   4.6g

Ingredients
1 lb. Brussels sprout, halved lengthwise
3 tbsp olive oil
1/2 tbsp salt
6 grinds black pepper
1 bosc pear, halved lengthwise and cored
1/4 C. shelled pistachios, chopped
1/2 large lemon, juice

Directions
1. Before you do anything, preheat the oven to 425 F.
2. Get a large baking tray: Toss in it the brussels sprouts with olive oil salt and pepper.
3. Flip them so all the brussels sprouts cut upside facing down. Bake them for 21 min.
4. Flip the brussels sprouts halves and decrease the oven temperature to 375 F.
5. Bake them for 9 min. Sprinkle the pistachios on top and bake them for 6 min.
6. Transfer the mixture to a serving bowl. Drizzle over them the lemon juice and stir them to coat.
7. Adjust the seasoning of your salad then serve it warm.
8. Enjoy.

BRUSSEL SPROUTS
with Berries

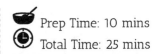

Prep Time: 10 mins
Total Time: 25 mins

Servings per Recipe: 4
Calories   73.0
Fat   4.8g
Cholesterol   0.0mg
Sodium   160.6mg
Carbohydrates   7.1g
Protein   1.9g

Ingredients
1 (10 oz.) packages Brussels sprouts,
trimmed
1/2 C. dried cranberries
2 tbsp lemon juice
4 tbsp olive oil
1/4 tbsp salt
1/4 tbsp ground pepper

Directions
1. Cut two slices in the shape on X in the bottom of each brussels sprout.
2. Prepare a steamer. Cook in it the brussels sprouts for 14 to 16 min.
3. Get a large mixing bowl: Mix in it the cranberries with lemon juice, oil, salt, and pepper.
4. Stir in the brussels sprouts and serve them immediately.
5. Enjoy.

Brussel Sprouts
with Spicy Mayo

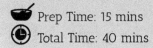 Prep Time: 15 mins
Total Time: 40 mins

Servings per Recipe: 2
Calories   196.3
Fat   10.9g
Cholesterol   7.6mg
Sodium   256.7mg
Carbohydrates   23.1g
Protein   6.0g

Ingredients
1 lb. Brussels sprout, trim ends only and
leave whole
olive oil
salt and pepper
Aioli
4 tbsp mayonnaise
1 - 2 tbsp sriracha sauce

Directions
1. Before you do anything, preheat the oven to 350 F.
2. Stir the brussels sprouts with olive oil, a pinch of salt and pepper on a baking tray.
3. Bake them for 22 to 26 min.
4. Get a mixing bowl: Whisk in it the sriracha with mayo. Serve it with the brussels sprouts.
5. Enjoy.

ORIENTAL
Brussel Sprouts Sampler

Prep Time: 15 mins
Total Time: 30 mins

Servings per Recipe: 4
Calories	170.9
Fat	8.2g
Cholesterol	0.4mg
Sodium	301.3mg
Carbohydrates	21.8g
Protein	6.4g

Ingredients

1 lb. Brussels sprout, trimmed and chopped
1 lb. asparagus, trimmed and chopped
1 red bell pepper, seeded and chopped
1 tbsp garlic, chopped
2 tbsp olive oil
1/4 tbsp seasoning salt
1 C. water
1/4 C. hoisin sauce
1 tbsp sweet chili sauce

Directions

1. Place a large skillet over medium heat. Heat in it the oil.
2. Cook in it the garlic for 60 sec. Stir in the veggies with a pinch of salt.
3. Cook them for 6 min. Stir in the water and cook them for an extra 6 min.
4. Add the hoisin sauce with chili sauce. Serve them hot.
5. Enjoy.

Vegetarian
Brussel Sprouts Platter

Prep Time: 10 mins
Total Time: 25 mins

Servings per Recipe: 4
Calories   230.4
Fat   17.8g
Cholesterol   15.2mg
Sodium   216.3mg
Carbohydrates   14.0g
Protein   7.2g

Ingredients

7 oz. extra firm tofu, cubed
10 Brussels sprouts
1/3 C. walnuts
4 -6 garlic cloves, peeled
1/4 C. cilantro, minced
1 tbsp lemon juice
1/4 tbsp red pepper flakes

1/4 tbsp salt
1 tbsp olive oil
2 tbsp butter
2 tbsp brown sugar

Directions

1. Prepare the brussels sprouts by following the instructions on the package.
2. Place a large pan over medium heat. Heat in it the oil.
3. Cook in it the garlic for 60 sec. Stir in the butter, brown sugar, nuts, and chili.
4. Add the tofu and cook them until it becomes sticky and golden brown.
5. Stir in the brussels sprouts with cilantro, lemon juice, a pinch of salt and pepper.
6. Serve them hot with some rice.
7. Enjoy.

SKILLET
Brussel Sprouts

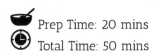

Prep Time: 20 mins
Total Time: 50 mins

Servings per Recipe: 6
Calories   105.3
Fat   4.8g
Cholesterol   0.0mg
Sodium   114.1mg
Carbohydrates   15.5g
Protein   1.7g

Ingredients
2 tbsp butter
2 tbsp walnut oil
1 large onion, peeled, halved and sliced
1/4 tbsp salt
1/4-1/2 tbsp pepper
4 -6 C. shredded cabbage
1 apple, cored and shredded
2 C. shredded Brussels sprouts
1 C. apple juice

2 garlic cloves, minced
1/4 tbsp ground allspice
1 tbsp dried parsley flakes

Directions
1. Before you do anything, preheat the oven to 350 F.
2. Place a large skillet over medium heat. Heat in it the butter with oil.
3. Cook in it the onion for 6 min while stirring it often. Add to it a pinch of salt and pepper.
4. Lower the heat and stir in the garlic with shredded apple. Cook them for 1 min.
5. Stir in the rest of the ingredients. Spoon the mixture to a greased baking dish.
6. Bake it for 20 to 22 min then serve it hot.
7. Enjoy.

Istanbul
Café Brussel Sprouts

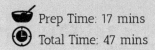

Prep Time: 17 mins
Total Time: 47 mins

Servings per Recipe: 4
Calories	156.1
Fat	7.5g
Cholesterol	0.0mg
Sodium	31.5mg
Carbohydrates	20.8g
Protein	4.6g

Ingredients
16 oz. Brussels sprouts
2 tbsp olive oil
8 white pearl onions, halved
2 garlic cloves, chopped
2 tbsp tomatoes, crushed
1 tbsp paprika
1 pepper, diced, cubanelle

1 tomatoes, peeled, diced
10 mixed mushrooms, halved
1/3 C. water
1 tbsp basil
salt
1/4 tbsp pepper

Directions
1. Bring a large salted pot of water to a boil. Cook in it the brussels sprouts for 4 min.
2. Drain them and place them aside.
3. Place a large pan over medium heat. Heat in it the oil. Cook in it the onion for 3 min.
4. Add the garlic and cook them for 1 min.
5. Stir in the remaining ingredients. Cook them for 12 min while adding more water if needed.
6. Serve it hot.
7. Enjoy.

COUNTRY
Pistachio Blended Sprouts

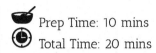
Prep Time: 10 mins
Total Time: 20 mins

Servings per Recipe: 4
Calories   139.5
Fat   14.0g
Cholesterol   30.5mg
Sodium   2.3mg
Carbohydrates   3.0g
Protein   1.4g

Ingredients

2 dozen Brussels sprouts, trimmed and
halved
4 tbsp unsalted butter
3 tbsp chopped onions
1 garlic clove
2 tbsp dried thyme
1 tbsp lemon-pepper seasoning
salt and pepper
3 tbsp chopped pistachio nuts

parmesan cheese

Directions

1. Place a large pan over medium heat. Heat in it the butter.

2. Cook in it the garlic with onion for 3 min. Stir in the brussels sprouts with thyme, lemon pepper, a pinch of salt and pepper.

3. Put on the lid and cook them for 9 min.

4. Garnish it with cheese, and pistachios nuts. Serve it immediately.

5. Enjoy.

Homemade
Hollandaise Over Brussels

🥣 Prep Time: 10 mins
🕐 Total Time: 40 mins

Servings per Recipe: 4
Calories   462.5
Fat   46.7g
Cholesterol   255.9mg
Sodium   35.7mg
Carbohydrates   9.3g
Protein   5.2g

Ingredients

1 lb. Brussels sprout
Hollandaise Sauce
3 1/2 fluid oz. apple cider vinegar
1 shallot, peeled and chopped
1 sprig fresh thyme
1/2 bay leaf
1-oz unsalted butter, chilled

3 egg yolks
6 1/2 oz. unsalted butter, melted
lemon juice
salt and white peppercorns

Directions

1. For the brussels sprouts:
2. Prepare a steamer. Cook in it the brussels sprouts for 10 to 16 min.
3. For the sauce:
4. Place a heavy saucepan over medium heat. Stir in it the vinegar with shallot, 4 peppercorns, thyme, and bay leaf.
5. Bring them to a simmer and cook them until only 2 tbsp of the sauce is left.
6. Strain it and place it aside.
7. Prepare a double boiler: Place in it half of the butter and whisk it until it melts.
8. Add to it the egg yolks with the strained sauce while whisking at the same time until they become smooth and slightly thick.
9. Turn off the heat and add the rest of the butter. Mix them well.
10. Add the melted butter gradually while whisking until the sauce becomes thick and creamy.
11. Season it with a pinch of salt and pepper then serve it with the brussels sprouts.
12. Enjoy.

SATURDAY NIGHT
Sprouts

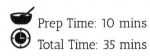 Prep Time: 10 mins
Total Time: 35 mins

Servings per Recipe: 4
Calories   93.2
Fat   6.3g
Cholesterol   15.2mg
Sodium   64.9mg
Carbohydrates   8.4g
Protein   3.0g

Ingredients
1 lb. Brussels sprout, trimmed with X cut on
the bottom
2 tbsp butter
1 garlic clove, minced
1/3 C. apple cider
1/4 tbsp ground pepper
salt

Directions
1. Bring a large salted pot of water to a boil. Cook in it the brussels sprouts for 18 to 20 min.
2. Place a large pan over medium heat. Heat in it the butter until it melts.
3. Cook in it the brussels sprouts after draining them for 6 min.
4. Stir in the garlic and cook them for 1 min. Stir in the cider and cook them while stirring until it reduces by half.
5. Adjust the seasoning of your brussels sprouts then serve them warm.
6. Enjoy.

Honey Nut
Brussel Sprouts

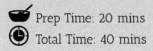 Prep Time: 20 mins

Total Time: 40 mins

Servings per Recipe: 4
Calories   244.2
Fat   14.6g
Cholesterol   15.2mg
Sodium   71.3mg
Carbohydrates   29.5g
Protein   3.8g

Ingredients

Candied Walnuts
1/4 C. walnut pieces
1 tbsp butter
salt
2 sprigs fresh rosemary, leaves picked
2 tbsp honey
Brussels Sprouts

2 pints Brussels sprouts, halved
1 tbsp canola oil
salt & ground black pepper
2 granny smith apples, peeled, and chopped
1 tbsp butter
1 lemon, juice

Directions

1. To prepare the walnuts:
2. Place a large skillet over medium heat. Heat in it 1 tbsp of butter.
3. Stir into it 1 tsp of salt and walnuts. Cook them for 2 to 3 min until they become golden.
4. Add the rosemary and cook them for an extra minute.
5. Stir in the honey and turn off the heat. Place it aside.
6. To prepare the brussels sprouts:
7. Before you do anything, preheat the oven to 450 F.
8. Get a large mixing bowl: Stir in it the brussels sprouts with canola oil, 1 tsp of salt and a pinch of pepper.
9. Pour the mixture into a baking tray and bake it for 11 to 13 min.
10. Place a skillet over medium heat. Heat in it 1 tbsp of butter.
11. Cook in it the apple pieces for 2 to 3 min until they become soft.
12. Stir in the honey walnuts with brussels sprouts and lemon juice. Serve them immediately.
13. Enjoy.

HOLIDAY
Brussel Sprouts

Prep Time: 10 mins
Total Time: 20 mins

Servings per Recipe: 6
Calories	123.5
Fat	8.0g
Cholesterol	19.5mg
Sodium	75.5mg
Carbohydrates	11.9g
Protein	3.0g

Ingredients
2 oz. butter, softened
1 garlic clove, crushed
1 lime, zest
1/4 tbsp allspice
2 oz. readily prepared chestnuts
23 oz. Brussels sprouts, trimmed

Directions
1. Get a mixing bowl: Mix in it the butter with garlic and allspice. Add the chestnuts and mix them well.
2. Spoon the mixture to a piece foil and shape it into a sausage. Place it in the fridge until ready to serve.
3. Bring a large salted pot of water to a boil. Cook in it the brussels sprouts for 9 to 11 min.
4. Drain them and transfer it to a serving plate. Top it with the chestnut butter then serve it immediately.
5. Enjoy.

Sesame
Citrus Brussel Sprouts

🥣 Prep Time: 10 mins
🕐 Total Time: 16 mins

Servings per Recipe: 4
Calories	9.1
Fat	0.1g
Cholesterol	0.0mg
Sodium	0.8mg
Carbohydrates	1.7g
Protein	0.3g

Ingredients

10 oz. frozen Brussels sprouts
2 tbsp frozen orange juice concentrate
2 tbsp water
1 tbsp low-fat margarine
1/4 tbsp toasted sesame seeds

Directions

1. Prepare the brussels sprouts by following the instructions on the package.
2. Place a saucepan over medium heat. Stir in it the remaining ingredients.
3. Heat them until the butter melts.
4. Add the brussels sprouts and stir them to coat.
5. Season them with a pinch of salt and pepper then serve them hot.
6. Enjoy.

SWEET AND HOT
Brussel Sprouts

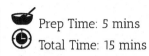 Prep Time: 5 mins
Total Time: 15 mins

Servings per Recipe: 4
Calories   75.0
Fat   4.0g
Cholesterol   0.0mg
Sodium   259.4mg
Carbohydrates   8.6g
Protein   3.1g

Ingredients
1 lb. Brussels sprout, remove stem tip and
quarter
1 tbsp canola oil
2 tbsp sweet chili sauce
2 tbsp fish sauce
1 tbsp water
2 garlic cloves, minced

Directions
1. Place a large pan over medium heat. Heat in it the oil.

2. Cook in it the brussels sprouts in batches for 2 to 3 min per batch.

3. Stir in the water and put on the lid. Cook them for 4 min.

4. Get a mixing bowl: Whisk in it the chili sauce with fish sauce and garlic.

5. Drizzle them over the brussels sprouts with a pinch of salt and pepper.

6. Stir them to coat and cook them for 3 to 4 min. Serve them hot.

7. Enjoy.

Southern
French Seasoning (Herbes de Provence)

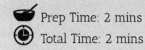

Prep Time: 2 mins
Total Time: 2 mins

Servings per Recipe: 1
Calories	128.2
Fat	3.8 g
Cholesterol	0.0 mg
Sodium	18.6 mg
Carbohydrates	29.0 g
Protein	3.5 g

Ingredients
1 tsp dried basil
1 tsp dried marjoram
1 tsp dried oregano
1 tbsp dried rosemary
1 tbsp dried savory
1 tsp dried thyme

Directions
1. In a bowl, add all the ingredients and mix well.
2. Transfer the mixture into a glass jar and seal tightly.
3. Store in a cool, dry place.

Made in United States
North Haven, CT
02 May 2022

18820817R00057